Crows on a Line

A collection of poems from the
Champaign-Urbana Poetry Group

ISBN: 978-0-9986710-3-1 (soft cover)

www.cupoetry.com
cupoetry@gmail.com

Cover image: Kathleen Louise Peterson
Interior design and layout: Lori Weidert/Friday Books

Printed in the United States of America

This book is dedicated to the memory of Pat Frick.
CU Poetry would like to thank her daughter, Diane Corean,
without whose generosity this book would not be possible.

My Mom

My Mom, she was a funny one
Who liked to draw cartoons.
She also liked to read a lot
And LOVED to play balloons!

She wrote some goofy poems
Very much like this one
She'd make up silly stories
and was always lots of fun.

My Mom she passed away this year.
It hit me really hard.
But what I remember most of her
Was her kind and generous heart.

I think, Hey what if I
Turn vinegar into honey
And donate some she left me
To a good cause for her money

Because she loved the arts so much
and for you, to which you strive,
to keep the joy in culture,
for me, to keep her name alive

All I ask is to think of her
and send happy thoughts her way
and maybe Pat Frick can be remembered
if only for today.

—*Diane Corean*

Contents

Introduction

CU Poetry was founded June 22, 2013 by a couple of poets hoping to make their poems better. We are committed to building community and strong individual voices through the power and practice of poetry, meeting once a week in Champaign-Urbana, Illinois, to workshop our poems and poems in progress with the goal of publication in mind.

We are an open group in a transient town. As such, we have seen many voices pass through our group over the last six years. The poems in this volume represent some of our members as of the summer of 2019. I wish to thank all the poets who contributed poems, as well as all the other members who have listened through countless revisions.

If you would like to explore your passion for words, join us as we share poetry, favorite authors, personal stories and how we can make poetry and the creative spirit a dynamic part of the community experience. Information can be found at cupoetry.com

—Jim O'Brien

soft and wet

Siraj Z. Ali

I am a Sword.
Born a Mass of raw Iron Ore.
Forged in bloody Battles of War

Songs of Glory the Heroes Roar,
As I Smash my Enemies into Gore.
Their Comrades singing nevermore

Tonight,
I wish I was a sponge,
a washcloth
soft and wet
lotion on ashen skin
so I could kiss Your tears away

under the gentle patter of mourning rain.

I wanted to write this poem from the point of view of a violent character wishing to be kinder and gentler. I played around with capitalization and the discrepancy between harsh and soft vowels to differentiate the difference between the character's nature and what he or she wants to be.

Sparks and Bones

Mary Barham

A careless spark
made love with dry straw
An ambitious flicker
lit the window pane
As a wandering traveler
came walking with singular purpose toward the embers
He hurried into the burning house
and rescued a damsel
A damsel crying for her hero
Her spirit was torn with faltering steps
Can this be real?

In his arms she wilted like the clouds,
smelling his rain soaked hair
and arms all sotted with ferns and mud
They scurried far from danger

Looking back like Lot's wife
she wondered and noticed
the fire's palette of ruin
was it the fire identical that long ago
had stormed the castle?
Its scorching red flames turned to purple
disintegrated ruminations
to blackened bones and ashes

This poem is mythological to me and evokes images of fire, isolation, and rescues from my imagination.

Echoes

Cielo Ines Bayawa

I threw a pebble on this pond
And watched the ripples grow
Rings of rise and fell
Rushed to the banks, swell

Why do that? You asked
Why disturb a water's peace
It's calm, at least the surface is
A rare occurrence very short-lived

For ponds are busy beings, you added
Nurturing many lives in their bellies
The peace on top you think should stay
At least that part of it is calm today

I share your sentiment, you know I do
But such façade scares me so
My tiny pebble caused chaos there
But soon after, they all went under

I shouted hello at that plaza crowd
Heads toward me quite surprised
Numerous faces, eyes questioning
A stranger shouting at them a greeting

Again, you ask why disturb that sea
Such reservoir of strong energy
Great potential but unorganized
Not entwined, uncommon, unwoven

Oh that? I did out of curiosity
To see if echoes come bouncing back
But no response, not a single sound
A fallout silence instead crushed me

I smiled at a stranger on my way here
He pondered a bit in quiet wonder
A second thought might have struck
Have we met? He smiled back

Now they say that's a nice deed
He'll surely make the next guy smile
And pretty soon faces of passersby
Are all smiling not knowing why

I was thinking of my pebble and
        my hello
I've learned some things, I had fun too
Contemplating, I was smiling
When I met you on that street below

Although in doubt you mirrored me
Others copied unintentionally
Waves of sweetness rolled far and wide
On this ocean where no smile can hide

For You

Cielo Ines Bayawa

Write a poem. Keep on writing.
A thirty-word line
Or thirty lines all made of one.
A hundred stanzas
Or one made of a hundred lines.
A piece that makes the reader cry
And one that brings a smile
That makes the stoneheart fall in love,
Or inspire the meek to speak.
When your words are brave, lame,
    or offensive
Still, keep on writing.

Read your poem. Keep on reading
One that brings out a gasp or stirs
    a laugh
One that leaves mouths open, a
    pin-drop silence,
Or makes the eyes shut to darkness,
Pushes the imagination to soar
To the clouds above the blue mountains,
Or dive the trenches of the deep oceans,
To retreat to the darkest room where the
    night whispers,
To bathe on the brightest day where the
    truth hurts.
Read that poem aloud.
Shout it to the hearts.

And when you're done and sunset
    is approaching
I'll write music for them
For the words you put in poetry,
The beauty they conjured,
The serenity they brought.
Even the ones that lead to chaos and
    the ugly,
The revolutions and the butchery,
I'll write for each a melody.
Lullabies that will travel time,
Hymns that children hum,
Love songs in wedding halls,
Anthems for the men in lines,
Notes for the quotes hanging on walls,
I will sing them with ferocity and might.

One night I was listening to Billy Joel's "Goodnight My Angel," *and the following lines prompted me to write this poem:* "Someday we'll all be gone / But lullabies go on and on … / They never die / That's how you / And I / Will be."

Last Great Lover

Nikki Byrnside

I have seen you before.
We both busied our hands with another.
Though the thunderous pulse of
passion was missing, hidden,
I knew you could not resist
my whisper,
the warmth of my breath as
I peered down your shoulder.

I was eying you even then
when my obligation
fettered me to another.
Now I am focused on you,
as you lie here,
I anoint your toes with kisses.
Forever starts with the feet.

When the heat
rises up your torso,
my lullaby tap-tapping in your chest,
fingers find your calves.
Feel the stiffening in your thighs
weight on your shoulders,
hands round your neck.

I simultaneously fill and purge,
spilling intensity,
as you yield to emptiness,
peer into new dimensions.

Limits that you have given,
the lines you have drawn,
I push you beyond the scream
you say you can't transcend,
but then you do, and you endure,
as new boundaries are crossed,
new lines drawn.

You swallow my darkness and hunger
        for more.
I am violent, forceful,
strength that you need
behind the terror—
the certainty
that you are mine,
and this is our time.

Previously published in the 2018 Winter Edition of Rat's Ass Review.

Leather

Nikki Byrnside

Leather is a scent
caressed by sandalwood,
kissed by jasmine,
anointed with sweat.

Leather is a sound,
a moaning,
a movement,
hands that draw closer
to stroke the beast
about your shoulders,
your second skin.

A touch
is never enough,
that tough rawhide softened
to a pliable barrier.

Rugged obsession
that cradles you,
rides you like a saddle,
begs to be handled roughly.

Leather conceals,
shields arms and fingers.
Leather tight
around the waist,
thigh high, zipped, laced-up, bound;
teeth bite down
leather won't cry out.

Lick of the tassels
lash down quickly
with a familiar burn,
like a shot of whiskey,
fringe of the whip
that stitches a sharp euphoria.

Then maybe a touch
might be enough,
when guided by your hands,
leather yields to your arms
and whispers
as you walk away.

Previously published in Voice of Eve, *Issue 10.*

Cancer Art

Sheri Daley

As deadly seriously suggested, here is,
obscenely, the first poem in a not-series
to capitalize on my son's Suffering.
For what purpose? To what end? Uttering
syllables of poetry? To collect samples to distill
his exquisite, inextinguishable pain, possibil-
ity of dying—down to this nada, this nil,

this *ce rien* de nothing, pathetic linguistic crap
exploiting pity for artistic gain? Perhaps
I will twist the experience; alter the facts;
dupe my audience with trumped-up, manufac-
tured claptrap, concocted sincerity; sell a fake act
so finely crafted, so finely polished
it will finally finally get published!

Then all the world will know
I made it. That's that. And I will crow
like a rooster, cock a doodle-doo, at first light
while I watch my son writhe in pain, turn white.
None of this is right. But somehow all that matters
days upon nights upon days, on end, of sleepless hours
is how to use this excruciating experience to write?

Of course poetry can transmogrify anything.
Take the sinful apple, decadent peach; chemo or dying.
Grab the nearest tragedy;
nothing's too sacredy
to trot out upon the predatory page,
jot profitable words as a crafty sage
and cast into Poetry human terror and rage.

Shipwrecked

Sheri Daley

Flung and flown, hitting wave after smashing tidal wave,
salt singeing eyeballs, mouth and nostrils grasping at air,
I made it, with an unknown strength, to the rocky shores
where stood a fortress, pillars and walls reinforced
with ancient Hatra towers, the fortified city that repelled
so many Roman invasions. Standing there, drenched,
on the store mat at the cash register, I dripped
all over the floor, almost collapsing from the exhaustion
of closing the gap from you to door, the proximity
imploding my neurotransmitters. I could have thrown

my arms around you from behind and squeezed
till asphyxiating death usurped me. I could have pressed
my lips to the nape of your naked neck; smelt
your unwashed, silky sleek hair; felt your fuzzy beard
nuzzling my throat, my chin, my cheek, my lash-breezed
eyelids; sensory signals snaking into wide-open, doorless
orifices. Ears. Nose. Skin. I could have inhaled
your pheromone-deluged being, like a last breath, for life,
even through sheer stone—the eyes that shone
on the five-legged sphinx of Nimrud. I will be
your *lamassu*. I will be the ancient Assyrian ruins
no one can save from the wreckage of time,
of war, of hate, of greed, of human hegemony.
Engrave this image, bury it under the threshold
of your entranceway. Watch me from every angle:
Am I walking or am I standing still?

Your honeyed, oily, creamy voice calling
my Christian name—the sweet, susurrating sound
like a *hush* parting your lips…*Sheri*…softly singing
like Sirens, to brain-bashing rock-crashing death
below—swallows my mind, my sanity whole.

All the shame that drowned so many earlier days.
Then came the anger that strangled the shame.
Now forgiveness wants to wash all that anguish away
while hormones act like nothing at all has changed?

I will make my way back from deep in the interior,
where abandonment, isolation, and confinement
keep an old Minotaur, sad, lonely, angry, broken
down and poor. I will emerge from the labyrinth
seeking new light, as a baby being born. I will learn
to use paper currency to navigate this violent storm.

Today, I Died

Ja Nelle Davenport-Pleasure

Today I died,
I looked over that casket and kissed your forehead knowing I will never see
   you again.
I wept.
I couldn't tell you how long I stood by your casket. It felt like an eternity.
You never opened your eyes, and your chest wasn't moving.
Your face, it was cold and damp. You didn't look peaceful.
You looked more like you wanted to stay around a little longer, and you were
   forced out.
I looked out into the crowd to see if I could find a sympathetic face.
None were to be found instead, I saw smiles, and heard laughter.
I saw people pointing and even clapping. What the hell was going on?
I say, where is your respect for the dead?
I scream why the fuck are you clapping?
I start crying and yelling and throwing flowers.
Swinging at the air, that is until you showed up.
I could see the pain within your eyes and the faint smile that crossed your lips.
You gently put your hands on my shoulders and pulled me closer to you.
My subtle crying turned to sobbing and wailing.
You just held me without judgement, without words until I disappeared and we
   were one.
Your eyes flickered and the blindness subsided, now I could see what everyone
   else saw.

The shell in the casket was the old me.
The me that was bitter and broken and angered by her circumstances me.
The old me that was so deeply rooted in her own despair.
The one who drugged others down with her to wallow in self pity.
That woman's skin was withered and scaly, she was bruised in the worst
    way imaginable.
You do realize they weren't clapping because she was gone.
They were clapping because you came to a place of peace about her.
You grieved her.
You let her go.
I turned around to the embraces of so many people that have been waiting for
    me to emerge from my hollow shell.
I begin to sob and within an instant, I was held and loved on.
I thought it was a dream and that at any moment I would awaken.
The crazy thing was I wasn't physically asleep.
I turned one last time to kiss the coffin as the pallbearers rolled the casket away.
Doors opened and the light came through.
I breathed clean air for the first time.
I took my future by the hand and we walked out behind the casket, heads held high.
As the past closed behind us.
I was bruised no more.
The smile on my face broaden,
and I strolled on.

The back story for Today I Died *came from a time in my life where I had to really
look at all the blessings I had in my life, and put behind me all of the negative things
I experienced. I took responsibility for my part in my misfortune and saw that once I
buried the past and pressed on towards my future, things in my life began to turn around,
and I began to life my best life. I buried that part of me, and blessed it and wished it well,
and then moved into my future without all the baggage. It was a wonderful and painful
lesson to learn; thus the poem was born.*

Living Libraries

Ja Nelle Davenport-Pleasure

What happened to us?

When did it become a thing to throw our elders away?

Lock them up in homes, or hide them in back rooms because we just can't "deal with them" today.

The living breathing libraries, chocked full of lessons, stories, proverbs, warnings… and encouragement.

When did we get so high and mighty, like we've walked the earth and done something?

Like we've experienced life.

I can hear my elders say "Girl you ain't nothing but 40 you ain't fully lived yet."

True.

I've got some living yet to do.

You know what,

I miss my grandma.

I miss moments of lessons that I wouldn't of forgotten, had I taken a few moments to sit still and really listen.

I would have avoided that cold marriage.

Those broken friendships…

Ok well maybe not, but I would at least had the tools to deal with them better.

You know what I miss most?

Sounds from her throat, that woman could sang y'all.

Her songs made you cry, laugh, and even slap you Mama

(for the record, I never slapped my mama. Shidddd I was still trying to keep all my teeth)

But her voice made you forget about the pain and it rejoiced with you.

Her voice carried you when you were unable to walk.

She carried the power of life and death in her voice.

You know what else I remember?

The smells (Sniffs air)

Can you smell it?

I'm talking Cornbread, Dressing, Greens, Baked Mac and cheese, Sausage bread, African peanut stew, Pecan pie, Pound cake. (Smacks lips)

Her food brought healing to your heart, and a balm for your soul, but you don't have to take my word for it.

Just ask the folks that showed up at her funeral. The will vouch for me.

Now her lessons didn't just stop at a few words and some piled high plates.

She was human, with faults, and worries like the rest of us.

No pedestal for her.

What she was, was my own mini library.

The best place to get a cup of coffee, pull out a book and just relax and relish in things
    I couldn't quite comprehend.
She was a museum, where I could observe the Marvels of preserved works and tell the
    Lil ones to hush or slow down when they were going too fast.
She was that shell on the beach too beautiful to disturb.
I find myself looking for her today.
I can't seem to find her face in the crowd anymore.
She's been replaced with these 30-something grandmas that have to get they nails
    and hair done every week.
She ain't got time for that cup of coffee cause her boo thang is coming thru, and
    she's gotta pick up the grandkids, and get their toys off the floor and make it nice
    for him.
She is no longer a monument to observe, and take in.
She's been replaced with Instagram pics and a quick like on your Facebook page.
And when her time comes no one remembers her home cook meals for they were
    long since replaced with take out.
No one remembers her face because it's been blocked out with her head in her phone.
That sweet but strong voice has been replaced with a robotic voice called Siri.
I'mma ask again what happened to us?
Have we've gotten so big, high and mighty that we've forgotten where we were all
    birthed from?
Where our lineage began?
Next time you're out, go in search of your elders.
The ones who can tell you where you came from and guide you to where you're going.
Grab a comfy chair, your cup of coffee and close your lips and open your ears.
Let the living libraries tell you a story.
Then listen, truly listen.
and you just might learn something.

---

*This poem was born out of missing my grandmother. There is so much wisdom I could
have gleaned from her had she not been taken from this earth so early. I was sitting in my
kitchen and crying, thinking about how I was raising my children and praying that I was
doing a good job, though I felt like a failure. It dawned on me that I didn't have her or
a mother to call up and ask for advice about this thing called parenthood. So I began to
look around me and noticed that most of the women my age were already grandmas, and
they themselves didn't have a clue about what parenthood was about either, and they
had questions like I had. Why is it so hard to embrace our elders and learn from their
mistakes or glean from their triumphs? One day maybe we will get it.*

Bouquet

Jane Desmond

A thousand seeds
lie behind the soft, furred mound
of each sunflower's umber center

but these will never fall to ground

Blazing petals,
bursting suns,
urgent yellow,

heats the room.

Standing tall,
these stemmed sentinels
suck up
clear water in a vase
sharp scissors' rapturous
victory

bringing sun to heel
like an exclamation point.

Last summer my partner brought home a bouquet of mini-sunflowers from the local farmers market. Amidst the clutter of the kitchen they stood out, radiant, and stunningly bright—a mini-miracle among the piles of mail, newspapers, and cooking pots, practically glowing as I placed them in a clear vase of water.

Unsung Hero

Vern Fein

Why would anyone dig up the graves of those atrocities when they have fasted from
    that horror
since Uris meticulously detailed Mengele's sexual experiments on children in QB VII?
I threw that book against the wall and read no more about those monsters,
saw no more films, not even *Schindler's List,*
though a commercial later revealed the red coat that will always haunt me.

One man, just one man, unsung hero,
removed my fingers from the eyes of my mind to look again at Buchenwald.

Buchenwald: where 56,000 people died.
    more than American soldiers killed in Viet Nam.
Buchenwald: all those attempts to architect the cells of Hell.
Those were real—tiny, bare, infested—not Dante's circles.
Death spaces for Jews, Poles, Slavs, mentally ill, physically disabled, gypsies,
    Free Masons, Jehovah's Witnesses, Communists, political prisoners,
    gays, sexual slaves, children.
Outdoors: *Vernichtung durch Arbeit*—"worked to death,"
and screams of pain in the "singing forest" when those men—*strappado*
Oh, I cannot write what they did to them,
and *Gernick Schuss,* 1,000 Russians shot in the back of the neck, and the
children.

One man, just one man. What can one man do?
He can tell a lie. He can tell a lie of mercy.

Like Shiphrah and Puah who lied to save baby Moses.

The headquarters at Buchenwald was dark on that rainy day.
The Nazi command had fled. They knew the Allies were closing in.
The phone rang.
How many times?
How many times did that phone ring?
    What if no one were there?
    But, he was.
A hand reached out.
The hand of one German man
who had the presence to tell the guttural lie of mercy.

(continues)

Command told him: "We will blow up the entire camp,
raze the rooms,
destroy the 1,300 prisoners left,"
including Elie Wiesel,
Elie Wiesel, whose luminous Jewish humanity gave lie to deranged Nazi fantasies.

The unsung (I sing of him now!) spoke:
"We've already destroyed it! It's done!"

(Oh, Sweet Lie!)

"The prisoners are blown up.
The evidence is destroyed.
We covered up what we did."
(as if the blanket of history could ever be pulled over that bed of horror).

The solution was simple, more brief than my imagination.
No reason to complicate mercy.
The Commander answered: "Okay, 'In ordnung.' Okay."

In a few hours, the camp was liberated,
 Weisel saved with the others,
 the Nazi command tricked.

The name of the one man unknown forever.
The result of one act can change everything.

I am from a Jewish background so am very much in touch with what happened in WW II. I found this true story in the Writer's Almanac *and decided to pay tribute to this man, whose name will never be known.*

Abe Lincoln Never Made It to the NBA

Vern Fein

Honestly, 6'4" Abe would have been a
    superstar center
in Dale, Indiana, which is what that little
    town
is named now, but was Elizabeth
when Abe worked on a farm outside
    there
and was 16 and sowed instead of shot
because there were no courts or hoops,
no Hoosiers or Boilermakers,
no NBA early entry,
instead became one of the most
    honored
All-Star presidents in our history.

No basketball then,
but gangly Abe could horseshoe with the
    best of them,
long arms stretch toward the stake,
long legs bullet the kickball at the goal,
big thumbs snap a marble true,
kids terrified when they called
    Red Rover.

No, had Doc Naismith
invented the leather ball
and peach baskets game back then,
Young Abe would have dunked
instead of speechified,
dribbled instead of traveled,
buck boarded to other little towns,
crushed opponents with his height
not his tongue.

Abe didn't win on the court,
but in the courtroom.
In the Capitol
dead from a bullet
shot because Booth
couldn't stand his team
to lose.

Buried Alive

Victor Fein

deep in the redwood forest
attending a men's retreat
standing before
a hundred men

he looks down
his voice quivers

been eating off the bottom
like a cat fish
sucking in any fuckin thing I can
to make it through another day

trapped in the hood
feels like a barrel of crabs
trying to scratch their way out of a bucket
know what I'm sayin

mama's an alcoholic
sis she
was raped by my grandfather
committed suicide

my brother's he's a gang bangin'
doin crack
sellin' drugs

I can't feel nothin
so I cut myself

know what I sayin
silence
thick as mud

This poem came through an experience I had with my son at a men's retreat in Northern California. Twenty-five were from the San Francisco inner city and received scholarships to attend.

Transformation

Victor Fein

My mother was a seeker of goodness; my father a collector and seller of ancient manuscripts. Having passed away suddenly a few months back they left me buried in grief and unattended affairs. At the advice of a good friend I decided the way to seek clarity and direction was to travel to the Amazon. I was told shaman use plant medicine ceremonies to induce insight into trauma, and release visions of the future.

Having arrived deep in the jungles of Peru, I found myself trodding through muddy trails that eventually lead to the Sibibo tribe village. Fortunately, the first person I attempted to communicate with knew a bit of English. She explained there were four other foreigners currently attending for the ceremony. I was assigned a tiny cabin where I could live for the next week.

A knock at the door brought me face-to-face with a man from America. I enthusiastically invited him in. He was on his fifth day in camp. He explained that morning gatherings were about purging, a cleansing in preparation for an Ayhawaska ceremony. We would drink warm salt water until we vomited.

This was the beginning of the cleansing process. That was followed by drinking various plant medicines, custom designed to begin healing the physical ailments that we shared with the shaman at our interview.

My first ceremony, I sat before the shaman in the light of a small candle that illuminated the wisdom in his eyes. I drank one ounce of the plant brew—threw it down like they do in the old Westerns. It had an awful taste, making it very difficult to swallow. The waiting began.

Near total darkness accentuated the intense jungle sounds. Creatures and insects each expressing themselves created a natural jungle orchestra. Intricate, colorful patterns began floating past my closed eyes. Soon a carousel appeared with small train cars instead of horses. I boarded one in hopes it would transport me to the town of insight. Turning the corner, the car slipped into a golden curtain. Before me stood a light green panda bear, its eyeballs rolling over like a slot machine, pausing now and then. If they stopped on dual images, the panda would speak a message. I received one: "Don't ever think you are alone in having deplorable thoughts now and then. Everyone has them. Only you can release yourself from their effects. Confront them with your mother's goodness. They will dissolve into puddles of conscious growth."

The panda morphed into a dusty, worn book. It lay before me on a delicately carved table the color of rust. I opened it. The text was in a language foreign to me. I looked around. Not far from me was an old man sitting cross-legged on top of a large toadstool. I approached him and inquired if he knew the language within the old book. Upon reaching for it, I noticed he was wearing a ring. The unique ring looked just like the one my father was given in trade for an ancient document. My father told me it had special powers. He never told me what they were.

I asked the man if his had anything unusual about it? He replied it made him capable of translating any text written throughout history. He told me to have a seat. Instantly, a colorful folding chair flipped open just behind me. I sat for a while, then began to become anxious, my leg bouncing to the beat of song "White Rabbit" going on in my mind.

He looked up from the book, stared at me momentarily, asking me to relax. Finally, he spoke. "This is the book of all wisdom. It was created by the holy spirit that has existed before the sun, the planets, the Universe. Before all matter. The page I opened reveals what you have come here for."

"Can you read it to me?" I asked.

"No, it is for you to ingest on your own. Hold the book, close your eyes and you will receive the knowledge."

He handed me the book. I did as he said. My father's image appeared before me. He spoke, "Son, you already have the insight and wisdom you need to become fully you. That is all each of us can achieve. Trust yourself; know you have within the keys to your ultimate fulfillment. Cast out doubt and uncertainty. Your leadings lie within. Follow your instincts, they know your path."

My father's presence floated off like a loose balloon on a windy day. My mother's hand appeared, beckoning me to give her the book. I knew it was her hand, she passed on to me a unique formation on my thumb like hers. She reached out her other hand. I took it in mine. The moment I took her hand in mine I returned to the ceremony.

Opening my eyes, I found the shaman sitting in front of me. The bright moonlight allowed me to see his gesture for me to sit up. Placing his hands on my head, he began chanting, guiding me back to present time and space.

The days passed quickly. The ceremonial experiences each taught me deep insight to life, happiness, and forgiveness. I left the Amazon having fulfilled my quest for healing past trauma, as well having clarity in making future decisions on dealing with the unattended affairs my parents had left me with.

While this story was born as the result of an experience in Peru, it is mostly fabricated by my imagination.

An Augustan Moon

David Hall

An Augustan
orange moon rises out of
golden, drying, dying corn into a
midnight sky, shimmering, vibrant
in this change of heat, cooling
with the coming Autumn
shift into Winter.

I sense this moment ... pregnant with possible
meanings. It soars upward, over me singing,
pleading for completion, and its communion.
Bless me, curse me now with thy wisdom.
I lie, waiting, listening, ... but, what I receive
is beauty, sweet, soft beauty, ... and, as my
weary eyelids close ... a train trundles slowly
by into the north, ... and with it, the vision
drifts
      away, like
           the drying husks ...
                    into ...
                       memory.

An Augustan Moon *comes from a partial line from my favorite poem by Dylan Thomas,* entitled Do Not Go Gentle. *It also refers to the great Augustan age of English poetry, which includes, the great poets Thomas Gray and Edward Young.*

Before a Night Snowfall

David Hall

For Ann Mary Hart

There is a weather in the world
that precedes a storm, predicts,
more surely than any forecast,
a precipitance of snow.
It is still, silent, solemn under
lowering clouds, a dark perfection.
A lull full of joyful portent.
A bright, uplifting, brittle cold
ripe for meditation, the cool inspection
of this world, this self, and life.

There comes a weather of the soul,
that predicts, unbidden, unexpected
at any age, but often late in life,
surely, our coming end.
It is a still, quiet, acceptance under
glowering skies, or in perfect light.
A glowing, soft, warm comfort
ripe for reflection, the strengthening
of spirit in preparation for this
transmutation into a new life.

Before A Night Snowfall *was engendered by stepping out of the Urbana Free Library on a cold night with Ann Hart, to whom the poem is dedicated.*

Both of my poems in this volume were inspired by lines from Dylan Thomas's poetry. In both cases, the appropriate quote is italicized.

Bone Broth

Ann Hart

white skin shows above a green collar
that sits below a mid-summer tan
greying hair cut short
for convenience, for control

a small white joint
nooked like an oyster
the top of his spine
neurons meet bone meet flesh meet life

she sees it as he bends over broth
wordlessly eating, spoon by spoon
his back—blank
she turns away, debones the chicken

first the legs, then thighs
moving up, moving meat
her knife work brisk
certain—with practiced hands

she cuts into breast, wings
her mind drifts to better times
early days, recalls caresses
surprise kisses on her nape

removes the neck, makes a notch
digs deeper, remembers
unexplained late work nights
       remembers
lipstick that wasn't hers

removes the heart, removes the rib
remember slights, remembers cruelties
feels the heft of the knife in her hand
thinks of expectations and realizations

(splits her soul)

keeps cutting, removes the spine
remembers the steel, feels the grip
in crimsoned hands
remembers his back turned

remembers his back is turned

Things Like That Don't Happen Here

Ann Hart

Outside my kitchen window
A starling mimics the sound
of the alarm on my refrigerator door
that warns me of impending doom
to my assorted cheeses and the
jar of Aunt Jenny's homemade pickles
I know the door is closed
I look anyway

Last night
a bear walked down my street
The few of us
The night owls
The mid-dream-wakers
called by restless nightbirds
perched near our windows
watched
as she passed under the street lights
rolling shoulders
moving her from shadow
to shadow

This morning
we gather heavy-eyed
coffee in hand at the school bus stop
telling the sound sleepers
the easy dreamers
the C-PAPers
what they missed

They ask if anyone saw cubs
and we wonder how she ended up
in our small midwestern town
We talk of calling the DNR
or the county sheriff
but no one will
what could they do, anyway?
She's probably gone, we say

Though tonight we will bring in the cats
Because you never know
You never know

Enough

Dan McGrath

The fields, now empty, roll past
frosted at the edges, they are lifeless
only stubble left, small yellow tips
of the once deep green stalks
that towered over summer

It's been awhile
so we try to catch up
my friend and I
as he drives along
the snow dusted blacktop
I strain to hear
his slow, thoughtful words;
he speaks so softly, this friend
whose red hair has faded
that he is nearly drowned out
by tires squeaking over dry snow
and wind against the windows

He makes small talk
of Annie, his latest of wives
of his job, the new boss
of doctor's visits
of minutiae

He wants only peace, he says
only comfort
and like the warmth of the car
in this darkest gray of January
that is enough

Waiting for Harvest

Frank C. Modica

My mind ripe for sowing and reaping,
I seek an open window, find none.

Fearing the night, that vague darkness,
I face an empty life at day's end.

No passion to fill my shallowness of heart;
Who can help me? I howl against the grain.

After Lunch

Frank C. Modica

After a croissant sandwich I'm ready for a nap
I drink the last of a mild Guatemalan cold brew.

The sun high in the eastern sky,
shallow shadows underfoot.

Who counts the years when they're happy,
holds onto their grief-stricken days?

Passion, fear. Risk, pain.
This is the life I want to live.

After a river boat cruise in April, I've been writing poems inspired by ninth century Chinese poets. Both of these poems reflect on my own personal experience, translated through the prism of those ancient Chinese masters.

The Art of Folding Fitted Sheets

Marva Nelson

frustrates me. It seems so simple when I re-watch
a host of instructional videos. Fastidious formless
women instruct in hushed ecclesiastical voices.
Hands flip, slide, fold the hooded corners.
Their ritual sheet taming looks solemnic,
prayerful, yet antiseptic. Just like the bus driver,
traveling preacher who tells me that he's blessed
each day when I say, Good morning.
He eyeballs me every day, inhales—holds his breath—
for what seems an eternity as we wait for the clink
and clatter of my coins to make their way to the bottom.
He wants me to say the same. I simply smile.
How can I tell him about my anxieties and angers
about God? How I keep listening for
the instructions? How each day I wait
for the heady scent of Him?

Why I Can't Write a Poem Today

(After Reading the Grisly Details of Emmett Till's Death)

Marva Nelson

Because that one light hazel brown eye
suspended by one last nerve gently lolled
back and forth, when his mamma finally saw him.
The other eye, missing left behind, somewhere
in the shed where the men beat him to death
or tossed as a meal shared between the old
mangy dogs that didn't know and didn't care
about the difference between colored or white.

Because someone took an axe to the back of
Emmett's skull, then sliced it loose from
ear to shining ear, his scalp flapping
loose like the hood of a Halloween
costume that didn't fit quite right.

Because—like his mamma—I hope that Emmett
was long dead when the men shot him,
the bullet leaving a hole through and through
his cheeks, the wind whistling through the trees
witnesses, mournfully swaying in the August breeze
as the men tossed the husk of Emmett
up and over the Tallahatchie Bridge.

All because Emmett stuttered. All because his cousin
showed him how to whistle the difficult words that hung
up in his throat. Because he had to ask the white lady
behind the counter in the right way, how much he had to pay,
hoping that he had enough for the price of the bubble gum.

Fledgling Poem

Jim O'Brien

If you believe a sonnet can be
a map to the heart and that a lifetime
of love started with you kissing me
then you might also know the sublime
magic of the full moon shining down
on us walking in the silvery light.
You know the way my heart skips
when it sees your smile, hears your laugh,
wakes up in the night then rests peacefully
until morning with your breathing. You might
feel each day and night fly by like a falcon
returning to roost on the falconer's arm,
outstretched but not reaching, holding tight
in its glove, trusting each moment
as it lands, at home in the bond they share.

Chains

Jim O'Brien

In the jungles of Thailand
monkeys are dancing,
circling a banana tree.
And chanting,
lifting voices of praise and thanks
for the bananas on the tree.
High above,
a praying mantis holds still.
A fly, not a fruit fly but larger,
staggers its way across
a banana leaf.
With a snap,
it is gone.
The chanting
carries through the trees
free on the wind
reaching the working elephants'
ears. Elephants who spend days
carrying tourists and nights
in mahout's chains.
Elephants who cannot forget,
who know the chains can't hold, know
they can be free with the monkeys,
yet stay chained just the same,
each link cracking like a seed.

A New Prayer

Kathleen Louise Peterson

a new prayer
wakes in the wind
skims tall pine trees

few hear or see

prayer falls
now   like a rock
and there remains
energy slowed to
a dense song singing

prayer rests on shore
as waves of water sanctify

prayer waits
    chanting Om

A Platte River Story

Kathleen Louise Peterson

This story told to you alone who meet me here so far from home
is about my life and ghosts near a river wide and long,
past cottonwoods and racing trains, o'er sands, 'neath flying cranes.
In that place, 'mid prairie grains, a whisper of my voice remains.
A sound first heard by La Llorona who bade me come along
to sing with her a fateful song.

Like her, I wear a long black shawl and weep to grieve my past wrongs,
my children vanished. My comfort riding far from me is gone.
All night, some nights I gasp and cry, none know the simple reason why.
While under Hawk's keen watchful eye the bitter fruit of things gone awry
revealed when Red-tail calls in sharp response to this lament so long,
my river-wandering song.

Nobody knows, nobody sees the stirring world of these poor
souls who haunt as they walk the dark and misty shore.
I join them there when my totem raptor screams,
while traveling in lucid Nebraska Prairie dreams.
River sounds call grieving, distant spirits forth
from shallow waters when moon birds soar.

The Accidental Destroyer

Will Reger

agile ditchwater nymphs caught in a Schlitz can,
a hundred or more at least:

he poured them, algae and all, to fend in a jar,
to await the promise of their kind.

he planned to let them loose on the grass:
to stage a plague as exodus

what did the boy know when he
carried those creatures home?

how could he know life would grapple with life,
within its curvature of doom?

or what that struggle would demand as,
by fractions, tails absorb and legs extend,

reaching for breath in a world slowly soured by death,
until muck returns to muck and not even his promise remains?

———————————

This poem is about an actual event in my childhood, as I remember it. Hundreds of tiny black tadpoles carried home in a beer can, poured into a Mason jar, and left to fend for themselves in the garage, soon forgotten by their young captor-god. They did what tadpoles do. They got bigger and bigger, growing legs and fighting to stay on the top of the squirming mass where the precious little oxygen could be had. When I thought about them it again, they were all dead, and it has caused me pangs of regret for the last half-century. The Accidental Destroyer *was written, in a way, as an apology for the boy who did what I wish he had not done. The poem was written about five years ago and has undergone quite a few revisions over the years.*

It was submitted five times and finally accepted in August, 2018 by Cagibi *(https://cagibilit.com/the-accidental-destroyer/).*

The Magic of a Poem

Will Reger

Lettery crumbs litter my shirt.
I'm on the bus eating poems from a bag.
They are soft and chewy like shrooms,
dried and salted lightly to taste.
The girl in the seat across from me
wants to try one, I can tell. I smile at her
and offer the bag, she reaches in
with a delicate pinching motion
and pulls out something by Pushkin;
bites right into it without hesitation.
Before long, Russian words are dripping
down her chin. She grins darkly,
tasting sorcery in the snowy trees.

―――――――――――

This poem describes an event that never happened as I have related it here, but each of its components did happen at various moments in the past. A girl sat across the aisle of a bus. A something was offered to someone. She chose and ate and enjoyed whatever it was. Another someone loved Pushkin so much he memorized the entirety of Eugene Onegin. *And there is something about Russian woods that evokes magic. Mix that all up and add a spot of polish and you have this rather pleasant, compact, mysterious moment, in which people are devouring poems. A sort of homage to my love for Russian literature.*

The Magic of a Poem *was published in the* Broadkill Review *in June, 2018, and can be found at https://www.broadkillreview.com/single-post/2018/07/28/Will-Reger-four-poems.*

An Apple Eaten

Roberto Sabas

An apple eaten
is five minutes deducted
from a walk, lessened
by the economies of
choice and obligation.

A child raised up
is twenty years added
to the journey that seals
a person to
their purpose.

A life lived well
is a score or more multiplied
by the factors of wisdom
and sense applied.

A love returned
is wealth, divided among
the dead and the living,
of which was given freely.

I wanted to write a poem of general maxims idealizing my hopes, dreams, plans, and experiences.

The Siren Queen Sings of Silence

Elizabeth Shack

Last night we sang the sun into the sea
Hot sand beneath our feet stained sunset red
Glad sirens singing sailors to our shore

Tonight the stars don't shimmer on stark waves
Your voices stilled by sailors' strangling hands
Your bodies sinking slowly undersea

Tomorrow I'll sing anger from the shore
I'll shatter ships, drown sailors in the sea
To feast my grieving few who sing revenge

This poem was inspired by prompts in an annual four-week poetry contest on the Codex forum for neopro speculative fiction writers. That week's challenge was to write in free verse on, among other things, what it means to be still or what is sung to the sea. At the same time, the #metoo movement was prominent in the news.

Cottonwood

Ruth Siburt

This Titan was a sapling
when Grandfather bought our land.

Through summer droughts
and winter storms it struggled
pushing down, down
strong tenacious roots,
stretching sky-hungry limbs
closer, closer to the sun.

In time
Grandfather could light his pipe
and take his ease
beneath its sheltering boughs.

Then did he dream
of a yellow swing
and a laughing child
suspended
between heaven and earth
sailing higher, higher
in the rustling dappled shade?

I only knew my grandfather through stories my mother told. When my husband and I purchased the land Grandpa once owned, I found myself wondering more and more about this turn-of-the-20th-century man, whose tenor singing voice caused a friend to ask for my grandpa's rendition of "Please Don't Help that Bear" over that new-fangled instrument, a telephone. Something in me hoped Grandpa's eyes might be somewhere, twinkling a bit to see his great grandchild half-a-century later enjoying the belly-tickling usefulness of his planting.

Published in Alchemist Review.

Hands

Ruth Siburt

You said,
　"See how pretty your hands look
next to mine."

I didn't tell you,
　but even then I knew,
your hands owned the greater beauty.

Strong enough to work the earth
　until it yielded up food for our bodies
and flowers for our souls

Gentle enough to cool
a fevered child

Quiet enough to hold an unhappy
　　young woman,
　never claiming to solve,
only to understand.

Nimble enough to out-quilt me
three blocks to one

They slowed me
　when I would have gone too fast,
and nudged me
　when I would not start at all.

And when I remember
　all the times a touch of your hands
made me feel loved,
　I want to say,
"See Mother,
　how beautiful your hands are
next to mine."

Some forty years later, I am comforted to manifest some of the ugliness Mother found in her hands: a familiar bluing of veins, pronounced ligatures, and dark spots. These "blemishes" foster hope that I might prove as worthy a parent as she.

Published in Unity *magazine and* National Enquirer.

A Night at the Theater

Karl Weingartner

They say life is composed of youth, adult, and old age
For me life is a three act play:
  Before Alison; my life with Alison; after Alison
Now I am in Act III
The last scene is years ahead waiting for me, when I will be
    consuming supersize quantities of medicine
    misplacing my hearing aid
    motivating with the aid of a walker and later a wheelchair
My mind will be sharp, knock on wood
    No chance of dementia for me because:
      Christmas present from daughter Fiona, a
      glass jar filled with marbles
      words written on the outside with marker
        "in case you lose any"
But let's not worry about that now
    I'm still an actor in the next to the last scene of my Act III, and
There is living to be done
    People to meet and enjoy
    Things to learn
    Deeds to be done
Onward!

The poem was written in 2016, three years after Alison's death from cancer. One doesn't really "get over" the death of a spouse. Rather, we move forward.

For Fiona, November 2018

Karl Weingartner

Meadowbrook Park, Urbana, Illinois, USA
Half six on a fall morning
Walking solo
  in pre-dawn monochrome solitude
  immersed in the silent, dark
Starry lit sky reveals
  deer ahead staring, motionless
  on one side: tall pine trees stand in silhouette
  other side: mist-topped, native prairie field
Technicolor dawn approaches—

16 hours hence—
You sitting at South Point on the Big Island, Hawaii
My sunrise has become your sunset

You and Frank Sinatra
Both living your lives, doing it "my way"
The adult you are becoming, choosing to be
Fiona you are my joy

In the early morning at Meadowbrook Park, Urbana, Illinois, I often walk two miles through quiet, unlit, deer-infested, restored Midwest prairie. South Point, Big Island, Hawaii, is the southernmost point/location in the 50 United States.

Naked Before the Mirror

Jerry Wray

(The Ages of A Man)

He stands naked before the mirror,
searching, and searching yet again
for the first signs of manhood, unaware
of the storms the hormones will unleash
and of the many roles he will play.

He stands naked before the mirror.
He finally likes himself and his body.
He's no longer a gangly, skinny
teenager; no longer a total hostage
to the emotions that came with puberty.

They stand naked before the mirror,
his young son sitting on his arm.
Grinning at what they see—
they are still wet from the shower.
    He shivers
with the intensity of his love for his boy.

He stands naked before the mirror,
critical of his middle-aged body.
It isn't as toned as it used to be,
has a little extra flesh here and there.
He wonders when all the gray hair
        arrived.

They stand naked before the mirror,
his body sagging, bent by the weight
        of life.
His energy is waning, and his strength.
His son, now the pillar he once was,
is holding his elbow while he dries
        his feet.

He remembers yearning to be a man,
becoming a man, remembers holding
his son, his son becoming a man,
remembers the shock of seeing gray hair.
He doesn't remember wondering how it
        would end.

Until recently.

Naked Before the Mirror *is part of the arc of one man's life.*

Life List

Jerry Wray

Random selections from my life
list of observed human activities as
recorded in the *Field Guide to People*.

Student sleeping during lecture.
Young boy skipping stones on water.
Dancer pirouetting gracefully on old stage.
Gymnast rolling, jumping, leaping across mat.
Old man with cane shuffling along side of street.
Black couple in park dancing to music on boombox.
Woman with child in tow pushing full cart of groceries.
Young woman strolling along street, stopping to smell flowers.
Two babushkas in traditional garb conversing in Russian watching kids in park.
Young man performing traditional Deer Dance in dusty village.
Woman in nun's habit striding purposefully around lake.
Student with magnifier peering intently at small flower.
Two Maasai boys standing beside road in black robes.
Baby sleeping peacefully; mother is napping, too.
Couple contemplating sunset across calm lake.
Old man on park bench reading newspaper.
Young man in army fatigues weeping.
Woman sleeping in church pew.

The *Guide* has many activities I will never see
in places I will never go. The sun and
moon have seen them all. I won't,
but I will keep watching.

Poet Biographies

SIRAJ Z. ALI

Siraj Z. Ali, a Brooklyn native, is currently a Ph.D. candidate studying organic chemistry at the University of Illinois at Urbana-Champaign. He dabbles in poetry during the rare times he isn't in lab or nose-deep in the latest organic chemistry literature. He hopes to continue on to become a Professor of Organic Chemistry, while writing poems about his experiences navigating the academic field.

MARY BARHAM

Mary Barham is a retired Registered Nurse. Born and raised in Champaign-Urbana, she has three grown sons living in Chicago. She volunteers at a grocery store/thrift store called Salt and Light, has a keen interest in ancient history, and spends her time reading, exercising, and attending poetry workshops.

CIELO INES BAYAWA

Cielo Ines Bayawa lives in Champaign, Illinois. She is full time homemaker who reads and writes in her spare time.

NIKKI BYRNSIDE

Nikki Byrnside lives and works in Urbana, Illinois. She is a student at Parkland College, and enjoys dark poetry, gardening, and dry red wine. She has been a member of CU Poetry since 2014, and her fellow poets have been an endless source of encouragement and inspiration.

SHERI DALEY

Sheri Daley earned a master's degree from the UIUC School of Social Work at age 56 and became a mental health practitioner. Sheri studied poetry under Professor

Charles Sanders and poetry writing with Michael Van Walleghen as a UIUC undergraduate in the 1980s, earning a BA in literature. Sheri has traveled widely throughout the ex-Soviet Union, Europe, and Southeast Asia. She taught overseas in Malaysia and the United Arab Emirates. A mother of three children, she has been an activist in efforts to pressure the Illinois EPA to enforce removal of the coal ash pits from the Middle Fork River and to hold the coal company Dynegy-Vistra accountable for its toxic waste. Sheri has also been a member of Jewish Voice for Peace, advocating for Palestinian rights for the past two years. Sheri writes poetry and gives community readings.

JA NELLE DAVENPORT-PLEASURE

Ja Nelle Davenport-Pleasure has immersed herself in the arts for more than 3 decades. As an avid dancer/instructor, jewelry artist, recycled clothing designer, and poet, Ja Nelle has engaged audiences throughout the United States and internationally. She started out doing spoken word competitions at the age of 11 and used that platform to overcome her fear of public speaking. It was during this time frame that she rediscovered her love of writing. She strives to help all, young and old, learn to express themselves creatively through movement and creativity. She wants to show her own children that there is no box worth sitting in when others don't understand your vision.

JANE DESMOND

Jane Desmond usually writes non-fiction academic work, but, thanks to inspiration from Maine poet Stuart Kestenbaum a year ago, she began writing poetry as well. Since then, the CU Poetry Group has been a welcoming home. With their support, she has recently published her first poems in online literary magazines *Persimmon Tree* in the U.S. and *Words for the Wild* in the U.K.

VERN FEIN

Vern Fein, retired teacher, has been writing poetry for about three years and has been fortunate enough to publish nearly 100 pieces in over 40 different venues. He is an active member of the CU Poetry group and attributes a lot of his acceptances to the excellent input he gets from his fellow poets.

VICTOR FEIN

After 5 years of college at the University of Illinois, I opened a restaurant with the intention of creating an environment that would feel like a living room for hippies to gather and share ideas and build community. We offered the first vegetarian menu in the area. I closed the restaurant after 4 years to pursue the custom woodworking business, and spent 43 years of my life designing and creating high-end custom woodworking. My crew and I were blessed to create beautiful wooden furniture and cabinetry.

I have been married to my wife for 51 years, and we have a son that works with at-risk teens of whom we are very proud. Several of my poems have been published in *1947 Journal* and *Social Justice Poetry.*

DAVID HALL

David Hall is 83 years old and lives in a central Illinois town called Tuscola. He has been writing poetry for 65 years. His favorite poet has always been Dylan Thomas.

ANN HART

Ann Hart is a poet, writer, and teacher in Central Illinois. She enjoys reading, traveling, and exploring pre-1900 cemeteries. Her work can be found in many publications including the *Monterey Poetry Review, The Vehicle, Rattle.com,* and *The Tomato Slices Anthology.* She was the 2016 Winner Champaign-Urbana Mass Transit District Poetry on the Bus.

DAN McGRATH

Dan McGrath lives in a small town in central Illinois, nestled between vast stretches of farm ground and the floodplain woods lining the Sangamon River. His poetry is influenced by his geography.

FRANK C. MODICA

Frank C. Modica is a retired teacher who taught children with special needs for over 34 years. His writing is animated by interests in history, geography, and sociology. His work has appeared in *Slab, Black Heart Magazine, The Tishman Review, Crab Fat Literary Magazine,* and *FewerThan500.*

MARVA NELSON

Marva Nelson is a poet and essayist who once taught poetry in a maximum security federal prison and work camp. Some of her best students resided there.

JIM O'BRIEN

Jim O'Brien is a founding member of CU Poetry. He lives and writes in East Central Illinois, occasionally publishing under the name of James Escher.

KATHLEEN LOUISE PETERSON

Kathleen Louise Peterson lives in Champaign, Illinois and is retired from teaching high school art. Mother of four children and grandmother of three, she is a seeker, teacher, dreamer, visual artist, and poet. Her pen name, from time to time, is Vivian Ren.

WILL REGER

Will Reger is the inaugural Poet Laureate of the city of Urbana, Illinois, and a founding member of CU Poetry. He has a Ph.D. from UIUC, and teaches at Illinois State University in Normal, Illinois. Reger has published most recently with *The Blue Nib Literary Magazine, Broadkill Review, Zingara Poetry Review, Passager Journal, Eclectica Magazine, Cagibi,* and the *Innesfree Poetry Journal.* His first chapbook is *Cruel with Eagles.* He is found at https://twitter.com/wmreger—or playing one of his flutes.

ROBERTO SABAS

Born in the Philippines and raised on Guam, Roberto Sabas imbues his literary and visual art works with the color and vibrant imagery of the tropics. A trained illustrator, he cites his father's influence in art and poetry. His short fiction and poems are published in anthologies by *Devil's Party Press,* the *News-Gazette,* and *The Alchemist Review* (UIS). His wife and children are the main focus of his life.

ELIZABETH SHACK

Elizabeth Shack lives in Central Illinois. A member of the Science Fiction & Fantasy Writers of America, she has worked as a software copywriter, a newspaper reporter, a physics graduate student, and a tour guide at a NASA visitor center, all of which she's composted to feed her stories and poems.

RUTH SIBURT

Ruth Siburt is a freelance writer living in Decatur, Illinois. A "nontraditional" graduate of University of Illinois at Springfield, she was the first-ever recipient of the Lincoln Library Award for Children's Literature. Her first published novel for middle grades, Dragon Charmer, went in to its second edition in January 2019. Ruth's short stories and poetry appear in a wide range of publications including *True Story* and *The Alchemist Review*. She is a past network co-representative for the Society of Children's Book Writers and Illustrators; co-founder of Decatur Area Poets; and a member of the Illinois State Poetry Society and the CU Poetry group.

KARL WEINGARTNER

Karl Weingartner, Urbana, Illinois, CU Poetry member, soybean guy, retired from the College of Agriculture, University of Illinois, in 2014. He and Alison Fong Weingartner were married for 38 years. Fiona, their daughter, is 26 years old.

JERRY WRAY

Jerry Wray is a long time resident of Champaign-Urbana. He's been practicing retirement for 24 years and is getting fairly good at it. He started writing poetry only fairly recently, and he's glad he didn't try to make a living doing it.

www.cupoetry.com
Contact us: cupoetry@gmail.com

Made in the USA
Lexington, KY
06 November 2019

56640608R00036